The Red Canoe

poems by

Jeanne Emmons

Finishing Line Press
Georgetown, Kentucky

The Red Canoe

for Adam

Copyright © 2017 by Jeanne Emmons
ISBN 978-1-63534-291-8 First Edition
All rights reserved under International and Pan-American Copyright Conventions. No part of this book may be reproduced in any manner whatsoever without written permission from the publisher, except in the case of brief quotations embodied in critical articles and reviews.

ACKNOWLEDGMENTS

I gratefully acknowledge the following publications in which these poems have appeared:

Alaska Quarterly Review, "Red Canoe Having Ideas"
Big Muddy, "Photograph of the Red Canoe" and "The Red Canoe Wishes not to Be Red"
Paddlefish, "Red Canoe Goes West" and "Red Canoe Listening"
Siouxland Magazine, "The Red Canoe Contemplates Plum Blossoms" and "Red Canoe on Still Water,"

For their ongoing support and incisive feedback and for lovingly shepherding these poems from rough draft to completion, I am deeply indebted to all the members of my writing group: Nancy Braun, Steve Coyne, Tricia Currans-Sheehan, Deb Freese, Barbara Gross, and Marlene VanderWiel. I am also grateful to the following poets for their careful reading and thoughtful comments on my work: Darla Biel, Heidi Czerwiec, Barbara Duffey, David Allen Evans, Christine Stewart-Nuñez, Melinda Obach, Pen Pearson, Marcella Remund, Lee Ann Roripaugh, and Norma Wilson. Most of all, I want to thank my husband, Adam Frisch, and my children, Eleanor and Austin, for their enduring patience, love and encouragement.

Publisher: Leah Maines
Editor: Christen Kincaid
Cover Art: Jeanne Emmons
Author Photo: Jeanne Emmons
Cover Design: Elizabeth Maines McCleavy

Printed in the USA on acid-free paper.
Order online: www.finishinglinepress.com
also available on amazon.com

Author inquiries and mail orders:
Finishing Line Press
P. O. Box 1626
Georgetown, Kentucky 40324
U. S. A.

Table of Contents

The Red Canoe Goes West 1
Red Canoe on Still Water with Clouds 2
Photograph of the Red Canoe 3
Red Canoe at Morning on Still Water 4
Red Canoe Listening 5
Red Canoe Having Ideas 6
Bailing the Red Canoe in October 7
Red Canoe Smiling 8
The Red Canoe Wishes Not to Be Red 9
The Red Canoe Watches the Dock Removed 10
Existential Red Canoe 11
The Red Canoe in Snow 12
Frozen Lake without Canoe 13
The Red Canoe Watches an Ice Fisherman 14
The Red Canoe Dreams of Spring 15
Red Canoe Watches a Lunar Eclipse 16
The Red Canoe Hears the Geese Come Back 18
The Red Canoe Speaks Freely 19
To the Lake, with Red Canoe Adrift 20
The Red Canoe Is Jealous of the Red Wheelbarrow 22
The Red Canoe Contemplates an Abundance of
    Plum Blossoms 24
The Red Hibiscus Upstages the Red Canoe 25
The Red Canoe Gilds the Sunset 26
Red Canoe and Lone Cloud, With Heat Lightning 27
The Red Canoe Contemplates Ophelia 28
The Red Canoe Eavesdrops on the Writer's Group 29
The Red Canoe Startles a Muskrat 30
The Red Canoe Awakens to a Spider Web 31

The Red Canoe Goes West

She has hitched up her ropes and moved
to South Dakota, along with all the rest
of our belongings, the same way the canoes
of Lewis and Clark were urged west
around that bend, upstream, against fear,
against fatigue, with all their guides and gear.

Now she can be wilder. As weathered as
the empty pod of a catalpa after it has
spit out its seeds. Unregulated as red
dice about to be tossed onto the green felt.
Eager as a bottle rocket on the grass.
She's altogether as pointed and kick-ass
as a red leather cowboy boot—bred
for swaggering, sleek in the water, svelte.

Red Canoe on Still Water with Clouds

Below, the water is a sky so blue
the canoe's red might be a leaf
unmoored from the sumac, buoyed
by the pure float of cumulus.

Above, the same exuberance of white
and blue, but without the scarlet gash
of her body, empty as an autumn pod,
and the dock some poet has lashed it to.

Across the lake, the dark brush and trees
rise from their reflections, grounded
both to the hidden earth and to radiant
ideas of themselves, almost perfectly true.

Photograph of the Red Canoe

There is the scene, just as it was,
the canoe afloat on a sky of reflected clouds,
but missing movement, the faint undulation.

Even if she'd been bucking in high gusts,
she would still be still in this fixation.
A camera will keep anything

from dying into change. But where
is that disquiet of the mortal moment,
the uneasy anticipation of the light

vanishing in the next instant, the wind
picking up just now to unsettle the reflection
of sky on water, red canoe suspended?

Red Canoe at Morning on Still Water

Near the far shore the lake
flattens out. The cottonwoods
stand in the sun on their own
yellows and greens.

But in the center some
hidden current unsilvers
the water like the mottling
of an old mirror.

And from that troubling
wisps of mist move sideways
in stretched puffs of gray
as from a pipe.

The red canoe is tied up,
inescapable, conspicuous
against the soft wash,
a statement of pure fact.

Red Canoe Listening

She lists from side to side,
an ear intent on something
beyond herself—the shush
of wind, the honk of a goose,
the clamor of cottonwood leaves
clapping together, the lap
of water at the rip rap wall—
anything beyond the incessant
knock of her own starboard
against the pole of the dock
to which she's tied.

Red Canoe Having Ideas

Last night she rocked
wildly in storm, and
now she is still, holding
water, open-hearted,
harboring in the red slit
of her body a bright,
leaf-shaped segment
of sky. She might be
a woman into whom
her lover has all night
again and again
poured himself,
so composed she is,
low in the water,
sleepy, smiling

Bailing the Red Canoe in October

I ought to pull her in each night,
haul her over the retaining wall
that keeps my lot from
sliding into the water. I ought
to turn her over, lock her up.
Someone is going to steal her
in the dark. Besides, there is
the rainwater that gets trapped
inside her red walls, water too cold
to step into, even after warming
up all morning in the sun.

I kneel on the dock, let down
a bucket tied to a rope, and bail,
rescuing, one by one, each pail
of sweet, clean water from her hull.
Hand over hand, I pull, raise up
the burden sloshing, pour a bright fall
foaming into the lake, where each
clear gallon grows quickly cloudy
then runs free, stretching out
from shore to shore
becoming the greater body.

Red Canoe Smiling

She might be a mouth lipsticked
as red as Marilyn Monroe's,
slightly parted for the kiss
of the camera. She hardly belongs
in this landscape of mute gray,
green water, yellowing leaves.
She is shy but lacks camouflage,
so she must posture and perform
and be provocative, clamor
for the attention of strangers,
while all else is self-possessed
and maintains an enduring distance.

The Red Canoe Wishes Not to Be Red

The geese are migrating. I can hear
their incessant calls through the double
glass of my living room window. I watch
them surround the red canoe, who holds
herself aloof in the midst of their honking.
They ignore the way she pretends not to be
paying attention. How she wants them gone.
They trespass in brazen sashays to plunk
down on the grass, shake, puff up, preen.

The red canoe shrinks down beside
the dock, wants not to rock, not to be
red. If she counted, she would learn that
the flock number two-hundred and nine,
but she does not count. She cringes,
too conscious of her color to worry
about the numbers. She is trying
to hide her hull, to ride low in the lake
that upholds and exposes her.

I am the one who counts, dimly aware
of the clamour of Yeats' swanwings
at my back. I count twice, squinting
past windows. I lift my binoculars,
peer through the lenses, focus on red.
Before long, the waterfowl will leave me,
and they'll return in maybe half a year,
regardless of the slit of eye I watch with,
the light craft dying to be anything but red.

The Red Canoe Watches the Dock Removed

The outrage of her unmooring finally past,
when she was dragged onto shore and overturned
again for the long cold, she had at last
resigned herself to the unmoving
land, and lay at ease,
the red slit of her eye
ready to close
slowly into
sleep.
But then
the shouts of men
roused her, with their waders
and their wrenches, the nuts squealing
on their rusty bolts, the hammering and hauling.
The cedar sections, the red metal ladder, all
she had held onto in storm now laid
beside her on the grass
and she who
once was
berthed
is now
doubly unsecured,
her moorings all dismembered
in the November wind. Now she wants
only to drift down and down into forgetfulness,
to close the great invisible lid of her eye
for good. And so she waits for
the slow shuttering,
the cold, dark
sealing
of snow.

Existential Red Canoe

That child pointed to the canoe
pulled from the water for winter.
"The red Camus," she cried,
"is upside down!" And the day
was at once what she made of it,
authentic, free, abandoned,
entirely empty of anguish,
—Oh, upside down Camus!
Oh, Sumac turned around,
turned red across the water!—
all of a sudden stopping to be
this instant what she saw, what I
heard, brimful of both choice
and joy, devoid of all despair,
head back, laughter outpouring.

The Red Canoe in Snow

is not red, has become now just
the landscape, a cold, white,
casket-shaped thing at the shore.
I forgive her now for all
her flirting, her forwardness, the way
she wanted to nose into everything—
red bow parting the reeds, the hiss
of her hull interrupting the silence.

I want her back. I want to pull on
my boots, leave deep tracks
in the snow down to the bank,
where she lies by the hard, white lake,
brush off a handsbreadth of snow,
remove my glove, lay my palm
on a red the color of frozen blood,
thaw her with the heat of my body.

Frozen Lake Without Canoe

I have not brought myself to walk across the ice,
though I have seen the tracks of deer and dogs
and the ski-lines of snowmobiles. I know
it must be hard to a safe depth, and yet
I cannot help imagining
that crack, that give, the slush, the slip of the edge,
and then the cold rushing up my body.

I need something bright and waterproof,
with a bow and a thwart, a gunwale and a hull,
something the color of fire, to carry me
out there over the snow that covers the ice
that covers the water where the firm, silver
lozenge-shaped bodies of fish hang
suspended, hardly shivering in the cold.

The Red Canoe Watches an Ice Fisherman

She lounges on her side in a coat of snow,
almost asleep. Then a man appears
with a yellow pail, an augur. Something stirs,
and her frozen, hollow heart comes to.
At drowsy attention, peering through the narrow
slit of her eye, she sees that the man wears
a jacket of kindred red, that he bends and bores
into the hard white and punches through.

The canoe does not blink or shift position.
She is marooned in snow. Her dark thoughts follow
the weight sinking, the taut line's tension,
down to the muddy, sluggish, dreamy wallow
where steeled fish are roused to apprehension—
an allure, a sunlit smell, a quiver of yellow.

The Red Canoe Dreams of Spring

On a frozen lake, there can be no reflection,
no meeting of minds between earth and sky.
The snow on the ice may shimmer
under the light of the moon, but Heaven
is no closer, cannot marry the Earth.

The red canoe is lonely at the ice-edge.
She longs for the spring softening, the limber
dip and roll, when the body of water takes
the moon's form into its bed, eases her
from the rarity of space to the common
tenderness of thaw, and mingles with her
in the shimmer and motion of love.

She dozes and dreams she is the moon,
a crescent waxing. Coppery, polished.
Then she dreams herself skidding
headlong down the sky onto the ice.
She does not break. The lake goes soft,
takes her into its heart, strokes her,
rocks her in its arms. She feels
her blood heat up and move in her.

Red Canoe Watches a Lunar Eclipse

It is that time of night when the houses
along the shore seem to float, golden-
windowed. Night after night, the whiter light
rises above the rooftops, changing shape
as if to tease. The moon might bend like the curl
of a goosefeather or swell to an egg or, as now,
come up a round, flat disc, platinum and pale.

On the bank, the red canoe thinks she sees
a thin slice carved out of the light, a blade
of black. She blinks. Surely the dark thickens.
Lying on her side, the canoe is uneasy,
shivers and narrows her gaze, wants to make
herself small. Just so, the moon shrinks down
to a silver bowl and holds in her belly a bulge
brown as clay, a bruised remnant
of her old self.

She is pregnant with some darkness on her.
The red canoe is riveted to that light,
watches it pare down to a shallow salver
upon which a dim mound grows and bloats
as a dough rises, its yeasty mass overtaking
the dish. Soon the moon is but a snip of tin.
Stiff with fear, the red canoe watches
her thin to a slip of nothing, and then
sink into shadow.

Beneath that blood caul, the moon
still glows awhile, faint, a beaten copper ball,
sullen, full of the illusion of warmth. Then
the whole Earth shifts its weight. The red canoe
shudders, swoons, blacks out. When she
comes to, the moon is peeking around the veil,
a squint at the very edge. A slender wedge
of white begins to widen,
a hard, tight, smile.

For hours the red canoe has anguished,
her heart slowly sliced to a gash. Now
her nerves are raw. She feels in her very skin
how Earth's great shadow tarnishes and shrivels
to a shard of black, how cavalierly he steps aside
and glides onto the varnished dancefloor of the dark.
And now the moon is out of it—high, white, whole,
pure, alone, inviolate, herself again. Whereas
the red canoe is an open wound.
Will never be the same.

The Red Canoe Hears the Geese Come Back

A flock of them skims over the punk
ice, the jangle of that gang yakking,
drunk with spring, makes such a racket
that, sunk on her flank, lonely, hungry,
the canoe is yanked to attention. That gong
call slung out to bring a rank of monks
to morning prayer. Flung out over the bank,
the muddy gunk, the dog dung thawing.

She'll slide down the slope and dunk herself
into the slush, out of this funk she's sunk in.
She rouses up, aware of the wrong of being
too long withdrawn, wants to launch herself,
beat her paddles in air. The drum of the wings,
the throng strung out in vees against the dawn!
Glory, honor, laud! She gawks in awe,
longs to extend the red tongue of her body,
and honk and honk and honk and honk and honk!

The Red Canoe Speaks Freely

I took the opportunity of storm and dark
to claim my own voice, willed the wind
to flip me from where I lay, upside down
on the grass, felt the gusts drive me into the lake.

And there I was, upright, unbound,
bobbing against the shore, knocking
at rocks in the choppy water under the
moonless sky. For once, unobserved.

Empty-minded, I improvised. Without her
paddles muscling me toward her aims,
I drifted, spun, almost danced at times.
Each drop of rain was a guest in my house.

Come morning, my red betrayed me.
She found me wedged under a neighbor's dock,
rode me home, secured me with a chain
from further exercises in freedom and dignity.

To the Lake, with Red Canoe Adrift

I would like to gather up your water
and carry you with me all day long.
You would slosh in my arms.
You would saturate my dark suit.
I would take the elevator
to avoid spilling, and
in my high office,
pour you onto the floor and you would settle
into a mirror to reflect the trees and clouds outside.

In you, I would dabble my shoes
while reading my mail, answering the phone.
You would flow down the halls,
lap against the walls. I would forget
to fill in forms. Instead
I would weave, in color,
visions of the world outside.
In meetings, during heated exchanges
about procedure, people would ask why
the dreamy look, and I would steal a glance

at the glint and dazzle of morning sun on you
and the ripples knitting and purling the light.
And if the red canoe should drift into sight,
dancing aimlessly
on bright water, her cords
loose, frayed and broken,
I would swim out, heave myself into her,
kick my shoes overboard, lie down and float unseen

past papers, pencils, staples, books, copiers,
parking lots, terminals,
my eyes on the blue sky,
the occasional cloud passing overhead,
sometimes a bird, rowing.
We would glide on the smooth surface of you, and I—

though all my colored strands lay loosed and raveled
behind in the empty office, though my wake
bisected the glassy surface of your calm—
would write my name on her and lie
like the Lady of Shalott in that bright boat
that bore her body down to Camelot.

The Red Canoe Is Jealous of the Red Wheelbarrow
after William Carlos Williams

I have filled my serviceable wheelbarrow
with clumps of hosta and daylily
dug from the road side of the house,
have guided it, wobbling, down
to the weedy lakeside terrace
to do my transplanting.

The canoe is too still,
trying not to rock
in the water, pretending
not to notice.
But I can feel
her mood.
Nothing escapes her.

To her, the red wheel-
barrow is not the depend-
able implement I take
her for. The canoe sees only
the superior shine, the prissy
single wheel, the impression
it gives of a woman lounging
on the lawn, leaning back
on her elbows, one leg
crossed over the other,
swinging her slingback shoe,
glad to be away from the white
chickens that always set her off,
glad it has finally stopped raining.

And my red canoe?
I could write about her all day long,
lavishing attention on her, watching
the whole world reflected in the inch
of rainwater at the bottom of her.
But for her it is not enough.
She glares at the red wheel-
barrow, and she knows
she will never
be so red.

The Red Canoe Contemplates an Abundance of Plum Blossoms

They are enough to make her forget snow,
forget there was ever ice to force her
onto the shore. They are enough
to make her feel that the soft flowing
between her and the bank opposite might be
crossed without paddles, merely by
longing to nose into the white
fragrance already humming
with impossibly small
yellow bees.

The Red Hibiscus Upstages the Red Canoe

Inside the window that overlooks the lake
my potted hibiscus has been putting out buds.
I have watched them emerge and fatten and
grow long, and now one has finally opened
its red mouth and extended its tongue of gold.
I want to draw the curtains. I do not want
to chance a brief glance of the canoe
up the slope. A whole bed of scarlet tulips
would not upstage her the way this red does,
its singularity, its proximity to me.

The Red Canoe Gilds the Sunset

Inside a large opening in the cloud bank
is a small cumulus shaped like a jellyfish,
and four others, smaller yet, all backlit,
shining. The red canoe watches them
until they thin and dissolve to mere sky.

She herself is a freshwater animal.
She does not know how she knows
that the shape of a jellyfish resembles
half a muskmelon, cut side down,
its threads hanging, dragging seeds.

The sky and clouds hardly benefit from
such associations. She does not know
why everything has to be compared to be
fully grasped, why all has to be held
in a tangle of connections, especially

clouds, which change minute by minute,
no two skies the same, and seem always
dying to be other than themselves, always
posing, whereas in fact (she is sure)
they hold themselves aloof, free of desire.

She imagines something making all this
happen, transparent, washing around
her, inside her, carving out in her
leaf-shaped self a hollow place
for these crosscurrents to slosh about.

There. She has caught herself in another
net of metaphor. Her red lips curve upward.

Red Canoe and Lone Cloud, With Heat Lightning

The red canoe is unmoved, tied to the dock,
her ropes slack. All day long, the August sun
has evaporated her rainwater, and now
she is dry inside, cooling down as the day dies.
In a sky otherwise blue, a single cumulus
hovers above the east end of the lake, its domes
replicated in the still water.

Opposite, the sun makes its way down into the dark
trees, and for a time the cloud pinks and brightens,
so that its image in the glassy lake lights up
and flushes rose and gold. And then the sky
darkens down to lavender. Violet. Indigo. Slate.
The cloud dims to a ruddy smudge.
The red canoe nods.

Against the black, a sudden spasm of brightness, and
the lone cloud flushes, darkens, flashes again,
strobes, igniting and extinguishing itself
like someone in anguish, like someone
watching a lover leave the house.
The surface of the lake throbs with light
as if in sympathy.

No rain comes. Over time the cloud will move off,
and the lake, upon which nothing makes
a lasting impression, will forget it altogether.
But the wind has risen, and the red canoe
is aching, knocking against the dock.
Already a spider has begun to stretch
a bright web athwart her dry hull
and its threads will tremble in her all night long.

The Red Canoe Contemplates Ophelia
after John Everett Millais

On the bank is a shallow inlet where
the young willows and the reeds bend
like a proscenium, and the elderberry
drapes itself and its white blossoms
over a log and grazes the green water.

Pausing there, the red canoe has a vision:
a pale woman in full dress, brocade and lace,
floating on her back, her palms up, elbows bent,
trailing flowers and stems, her eyes open,
glazed, her mouth, too, open as if singing.

The red canoe doubts herself, questions
her sanity, wonders what unseen burden
she has in her to so trouble the smooth surface
of her mind with such thoughts, uncalled for.
The load shifts. With a lurch and a pitch
the paddle dips and pulls the vision by.

The Red Canoe Eavesdrops on the Writers' Group

She knows they are talking about her,
up the slope, past the terrace, the yellow-lit
windows. In the hollow of her hull their voices
sound. She resents the talk, knows full well

they are trying to make her other than she is.
She stiffens, wants to thwart the change they
impose on her, hates the way she has no say in
her own fate, not even her intrinsic self, her being

a canoe. Even her red she is doomed to, her
identity, her powerlessness, lacking engine
and sail, lacking rudder, even. She just wants to be
left alone, to steady herself against the waves

the speedboats make, to be tied up, soothed
by her own rhythmic bumping against the old
tires wired to the dock. Yet she knows
that all this talk and laughter at her expense

will culminate in those quiet moments when
the water will seem to rise under her, lift her,
expose her to the gaze of some singular witness,
as if a pair of binoculars swung to focus on

her alone, her canoe-shape, her movement.
Does she only imagine then that she is
remarkable, more herself than ever—more
than herself, her red more wet, more red?

The Red Canoe Startles a Muskrat

Silent gliding, then
the knock of the paddle,
Now a sudden splash,
wet fur coming to
hundreds of separate points
on a curved back.
It rotates, a spiked wheel,
dives, disappears, and leaves
the closing water,
ripples that crowd
other ripples, then
flatten to a soft
undulation,
then no trace.

The Red Canoe Awakens to a Spider Web

She can feel it shivering in the
slight breath of morning, between
the thwart and the rear seat, the filaments
radiant in that horizontal light, making
unlikely links, sticky seams in space
to capture the least sailing mayfly
of possibility, the most flagrant fantasy
threading its wings through air.
The maker not showing herself,
hiding in the dark, biding her time.

Jeanne Emmons was born in Louisiana and raised in Texas, where she received her PhD in English from the University of Texas. After moving to Iowa with her husband, she taught English and Creative Writing at Briar Cliff University and raised two children. Her move to South Dakota to live on McCook Lake and her experiences paddling her canoe formed the inspiration for these poems.

In addition to *The Red Canoe,* Jeanne Emmons has published three full-length collections: *The Glove of the World* (2006), winner of the Backwaters Press Reader's Choice Award; *Baseball Nights and DDT* ((Pecan Grove Press, 2005), and *Rootbound* (1998), winner of the New Rivers Press Minnesota Voices Competition. She has won the Comstock poetry prize, the James Hearst Poetry Award, and the Sow's Ear poetry award, among others. Her work has appeared in *The Alaska Quarterly Review, The American Scholar, The Carolina Quarterly, Louisiana Literature, The North American Review, The South Carolina Review, Prairie Schooner, The River Styx, The South Dakota Review,* and many other journals. She is poetry editor of the *Briar Cliff Review*.

www.ingramcontent.com/pod-product-compliance
Lightning Source LLC
LaVergne TN
LVHW041509070426
835507LV00012B/1441